Step Scenes of Life

By Dudley (CHRIS) Christian

A

Pause For Poetry©

Publication

Acknowledgement:

Special thanks to my wife, Marilyn Christian for compiling, organizing and finalizing the books of my collections. Her photographic and editing skills were vital to all of my works.

ISBN: 978-0-9916853-2-5

First Edition September 2012

Revised Edition June 2017

Copyright © 1971 by Dudley (Chris) Christian

ALL RIGHTS RESERVED. Any unauthorized reprint or use of this publication is prohibited. No part of this book may be reproduced or transmitted in any form or by any means, electronic or mechanical, including photocopying, recording, or by any information storage and retrieval system without express written permission from the author.

Cover Photograph: Lana and the Dragon Kite © Marilyn Christian

Dudley (Chris) Christian founded and hosted the first and only "PAUSE FOR POETRY" show dedicated solely to the introduction of new and unknown poets and their works. This TV series ran from 1974 to 1985.

An Opening Word by the Author....

Often people ask:

"How do you write and do you have to often rewrite your material?"

I have long summed up my answer to the above with the following:

"A Word, the written word, small purveyor of a thought, so like a thought, once thought, cannot be recalled, so too, a word once writ, should need NOT be re-written, for with such licence, we would but change ... the very substance of the thought."

... DNC©1970

Table of Contents

Woman Oh Woman..1

Visions Mere Of Life 2

In Dismal Darkened Loneliness.. 4

Again Life It Comes Eternal 5

There Is A Land... 6

Sweetheart There's No Need... 7

Oh The Mountains So Huge.. 10

To My -----, ...11

I Remember Your "Sheeet"... 12

A Soldier Sent To War *.. 13

Oh Canada I've Come To You.. 14

What Do You See In Your Novel.................................... 16

Life Is A Dream In Reality... 18

I've Searched and Searched... 19

As The Sun Comes Up..20

I've Worked All Day For A Living 21

No Darn Business Of Yours..22

No Fault I Find In You...23

When Life Brings To Me Disgust 24

Look -- Look -- Look And See 26

Iraq Is Like A 98 lb Teenage Girl * 27

A Picture Of Life Has Started 28

A Flower Is Lovely..30

Darling Please Hold My Hand 31

If You'd Only Be A Wife 32

How'd You Like To Be	34
Why Do You Descend So Bleak	36
Today Is April The Twenty Fourth	37
The Fall Of Snowflakes	38
Oh What A Way To Live My Life	40
The John's Graffiti	42
We All Must Do That In Life *	43
Hey Little Girl Tripping	44
Life Is An Empty Place To Be	46
Just Another Mock Trial	47
Today On The Waters I Sailed	50
Why Do You Blanket Me	51
How Old Are You	52
It Really Is A Wonder	54
What Is Right Or Wrong	56
Remember The Words *	57
Speaking Of Love	58
In This Wacky Wacky City	60
The BC's SC Shaft	61
Daily Prayer	62
These Prison Bars May Bind Me	63
A Crow On A Log	64
And Near Near Evermore	65
I Saw Three Fishing Boats	66
Cold Dark And Dismal Grey	68
I Have Leaned Against The Bough	70

She Smiled And Smiled	72
If I Should Die Tomorrow	74
With Scornful Eyes	75
You Are And I Am Not	76
I Am Sure You Can't Imagine	77
Oh My Children How I Wish	78
I Walk The Empty Beach	82
Glance Up You Auto Driver	84
The Bloodhounds	88
And On	92
Some Fancy University	93
"Ne Dha Wha La Wan"	96
Shocks	98
There's A Ring Upon A Finger	100
Players All Are We	104
'Twas A Balmy Spring Day	106
Pause For Poetry	107
Beyond The Far And Blue Horizon	108
Tiny White Cylinder	110
Ah Life What Has Thou Done	111
Once Again You're Painting	114
I Listened To A Man	115
You And I Old Faithful Friend	118
In Memory Of Randy	119
A Charmer No No Charmer I	122

Dear Reader:

Thank you for stopping for one short "Pause for Poetry" (page 107) wherein I pray my words will be a password to take you back on roads to flashbacks for a while.

" 'Twas a balmy spring day" (page 106) when "I have leaned against the bough" (page 70). It put my gaze "far beyond the far and blue horizon" (page 108) and I thought "my children how I wish" (page 78) there had been far greater moments to have spent with you. And yet, my friends, I wish "if I should die tomorrow" (page 74), I had had more time to get to know you better and to let you know me too. But thank you all for the appreciated moments, the unforeseen input and the brightening results your contribution did to my life add, "as I walk the empty beach" (page 82).

So as you, I hope, will do, come walk with me and wonder at the many scenes, which I hope you will pause upon and take a new step of what was, and is, my life.

Woman Oh Woman

Woman oh woman!
I have I'm told excellent health
I've riches I need not wealth
There's nothing there I need from you
You cannot give me health or wealth
You can't give me a home
You can't afford me warmth or truth
That I can't find along lifes road
I've traversed this wide world around
I've seen it in its full length
There's naught left of this lifes pleasures
That day or night I've not spent
I've found that I can find with ease
Each pleasure that you may give
I've found that nothing now remains
Which if sought from life life will not give
I've tasted all the fruits that be
From hell below to the high heavens above
'Till there's but one thing I you can give to me
And that one thing "woman" is love
So if you care to barter woman
With the one thing that you have
There's always someone warm waiting welcome
To share free that thing with this man

Visions Mere Of Life

You came into my life unexpectedly
Said 'Hello" and you were gone
Your name alone you left for memory
As on life's roads you hurried on
Who were you and where comest from
Did I but think thy presence here
Or mayhap I a dream in too long
I stayed and to awaken cannot bear
My mind it surely doth tricks play
When visions so vivid I recall
As thy form and fragrance ever sweet
Seems my senses to touch on all
No contact save but verbal given
'Cept the reaching of the meeting eye
Yet conversations drift back soft
To each word recall – I needn't try
Where did you go, are you really gone
Has cruel fate another slap me given
Has life once more out of my Hell
But playfully shown me part of Heaven
Why can't I grasp unto reality
Clear cobwebs from my deeper mind
See light where light's meant to be

And in the dark true darkness find
Why exist I in this euphoric state
Belief in thoughts – in visions – and in dreams
Seeing you here where you I imagined
Had once walked – laughed – talked – it seems
But unreal you – like my visions
Disappears when they I try to touch
Mirages on the backroads of a mind
That in a life of images – sees too much
Still above all I recall a name
A face that smiled soft and warm
A body which exuded sensuousness
As it brushed but slightly by my arm
A pair of lips that beckoned for kissing
Two eyes that tell the world of what's within
A voice which stays beating of my heart
While telling of a heart warm which beat within
These things I did not dream ----- did I
These all could not visions mere have been
These must have been part of a whole
These must be there for me to find again
For ---------------

In Dismal Darkened Loneliness

In dismal darkened loneliness
I sit and wait sound of your voice
Just passing cheerily by my door
Not looking out I see your face
Framed in my minds gold picture frame
With all the love that once it bore
Unspeaking deep within of me
Your words and voice echo again
And music fills my life once more
Then soft upon my face I feel
The fingers of your love filled touch
And you've returned to me I'm sure

I open my bloodshot tearless eyes
And gaze into dark lonesomeness
Pray that it's not a dream
My heart race with a pounding beat
My thought flood full my mind
Yet still alone the darkness scream
I arise and shake my lonely head
I pace the floor alone, alone

Fall back upon my empty bed
Gaze up at darkened nothingness

Listen to silence of – alone
And pray and pray for sleep instead

The dismal dark of loneliness
Deep falls upon my heart
I sit and await sound of your voice
Last heard when we did part
And wonder where you are

20/9/91

Again Life It Comes Eternal

Again life it comes eternal
To render me a grasp
Of happiness and joy
To show a flailing
Empty shell like me
That we need not hop in life again
Again love it comes eternal
To bright my days and my life renew
To lend a hand if willing I would take
But chance no given for just two
And let it carry ever
Onwards living loving so natural

There Is A Land

There is a land — there is a land —
There has to be a land
A land — such as the heart alone has seen
A land — where man is equal free
Where there is peace and harmony
A land such as which we of but dream
Yet I recall in my mind's eye
Days long passed and years gone by
When free we roamed in such a land ---
Yea, I recall those sweet old days
Glittering nights near moonlit bays
When I was there in such a land — as man
Then pray oh pray tell me e'en now
What land was this you speak of now
Where man was man and happy free
That land — was land unconquered by
The troubles of the mind or eye
Unmarred in beauty and in majesty
So far away tho seems the time
This dream remains so in my mind
And I but 'vision that again I'll find
Such a land — oh such a land
Yes such a land is there someplace
Where there exist one multi-race
Where love is writ on every face
Where life is love and love is life
Where night and day become as one
Where tranquility goes on and on
Where war is gone and so is hate

Where cultures do not separate
Where you and I and everyman
Doth live and love our fellowman
Tho now a dream —
I know it's real
For I have lived —
In such a land

Sweetheart There's No Need

Sweetheart there's no need for you to say
How much you'd love to go away
Cause your actions have long spoken so to me
You say that I no longer care
And that I wish you weren't here
But it's only your own feelings you see
You cannot see the hurt you've brought
to this sorry life I live
You are so sick within yourself you no longer care to live
I've asked of you dear nothing save
The little that all husbands crave
Yet even this you have denied me
With your selfish ways
You're afraid sweetheart to face life
To live and love and let
You're so all centered round yourself
You seek reward in all you get
You're neither cute nor ugly
You're not so smart at all
You feel somehow uplifted
Each and every time you see me fall

You fail to do the duties
Of a woman mother wife
Yet you believe my love will last
Throughout this heckled life
You would give me my freedom
Tho that could never be
Cause as your fool I married you
And your fool I'll always be
I do not crave for riches
Nor for mansions oh so grand
I do not care to live on filth
Or on the fat of this here land
I work my best each day sweetheart
Hoping you'd realize
I loved you then I love you now
You're heaven to my eyes
You've given me a child its true
Of whom I care a lot
But deep within my heart there burns
Desire for love you giveth not
God gave to you the body the health and then the man
To be a woman here on earth it was His only plan
You really are inhuman to deny to me this right
By keeping back yourself from me
each cold and lonely night
You could give me the love for which you know I crave
But in your selfish ways instead
you drive me to my grave
You use your lame excuses
you try your best to get me mad

You drive me to another, tho I go not still you're sad
You're hoping that somehow
someday you'll make me be untrue
But that alas I cannot be Because I still love you
One day when God is angered
we all for our sins shall pay
He'll gain His full vengeance, in time to come He'll say
Where is the lonesome talent which I to you did give
Where is the glorious right
of birth-from which life on Earth I give
You cannot then hide and say Lord
my youth and use is gone
My body groweth old and weak
my husband he's run down
He'll turn to you and take your child
as He's done so oft before
And you'll be alone so all alone
cause you haven't anymore
So open up your eyes dear and realize today
That the gift God did give to you
He too can take away
And when you hear no longer
A child's sweet speech and laughter
You'd wish you'd given unto me
More sons and more daughters
I will always love you
And wait for you forever
I hope you'll learn before it's too late
He's watching you in Heaven

Oh The Mountains So Huge

Oh the mountains so huge and so mighty
Are caressed by the soft clouds with love
As they silently stand in the distance
They're glad to see clouds high above

The water the snow and the sunshine
Reminds them that somebody cares
Like your arms warm around me did tell me
That your love would last through the years

But alas the mountains are standing
And the clouds still caress them I see
But I'm as cold as the snow on the mountain
Since you took your warm love from me

All my days are lonely and cloudy
All my nights the tears fall like rain
All my life has turned into Winter
All my heart is caressed with is pain

But there's a mighty mighty city
Gleaming so bright 'cross the waves
Where I had to leave you my Darling
For, for me, you no longer cared

To My -----,

If there is a Heaven
It is You
If there is an Angel
It is You
If there exists Peace on Earth
To give joy to our land o'erwroth
To share loves laughter as we ought
It is You
If there is a plan for man – It is You
If there is a reward grand – It is You
If there is a life beyond
After this lifes sorrows're gone
And pain is lost for everyone
It is You
If I seem to think too deep – It is You
If dreams they haunt all my sleep – It is You

If I find before my eyes
One day on waking an ultimate prize
'Twould be but one I'd visualize
It is You
It is You because you are
The axis 'round which spins my Earth
The plan of ages past and gone
The hope of ages yet to come
It is You we'll always find
First in our thoughts – First in our minds
The highest goal of any man
Will always be just You
It is You
For You are Woman

I Remember Your "Sheeet"

I remember your "Sheeet" when we first met
As you danced snuggled in my arms
And your "wait till I get my hands on you"
Accentuated by the gleam in your eyes
The soft warmth as you pressed against me
Your every feeling to me revealed
The sweetness of your tender kisses
Your free flowing wild abandon of fear
The purrs as you whispered so softly
In my ears till evening was gone
Your hands roaming over my body
As we slowly drove to your home
Then your exclamation of pleasure
When completely to me you came
Winding your lovely body around me
Calling over and over my name
The warm wonder and beauty of passion
As we made love for hours on end
Each time completed in ecstasy
Just to hear your soft whisper "again"
Then lying together in fulfillment
Your still wet body soft by my side
Wrapped in the embrace of each other

Lip to lip, toe to toe, thigh to thigh
The beauty and warmth of true passion
Which alone brings fulfillment to love
Is a feeling few find till it's too late
To grasp and keep it ever like now
So many men have gone right on living
With a life and a wife who's so cold
That making love becomes but a duty
Never having had a chance passion to hold
Much more than a body just lying
As a receptacle given by duty bound
Loves true passion gives wild abandon
Leaping life's inhibitions with a bound
Removing all that held one restricted
Afraid to enjoy full love and life
This passion given free by the mistress
Of the man refused it by his wife

> A soldier sent to war,
> like any person offered drugs
> can just say 'NO'

Oh Canada I've Come To You

Oh Canada,

Oh Canada I came to you with open arms

With wisdom words

With new things learnt

With things I've heard

I've come to you with writings new

I've come to you to give my best

I've come to you

Oh Canada

Oh Canada

Oh Canada I've come to you with love of life

I've learned to live with you

Thru hurt

Thru pain and strife

I've tried my best you to understand

I've tried my best oh Canada

To make you my land

Oh Canada I came to you to find again

A way of life to share full with my fellowmen

You taught me that you cared not to see

You showed no help

No love -- and no sympathy

Oh Canada I came to you alone

Intent

Content

To make you my home

Full eager, willing

To try, with you to abide

But all my dreams

You have now cast aside

Oh Canada alas from you I go

I go back back to a land

Warmer that I used to know

A land where what I offer

Won't be turned back

Oh Canada

You've cast me out for I was black

What Do You See In Your Novel

What do you see in your novel

By which you so deeply are moved

Has Menfreya given thoughts to you

What from Miss Holt have you learned

With your hand upon your chin dear

You so deep and thoughtfully sit

Tell me my love what interests you

In that novel with which you sit

As your coat limply hangs on your shoulders

And you cross your legs shapely and fair

As you glance now across the blue waters

Do you remember that I am here

Has your thoughts of coming motherhood

Been touched by the book which you read

What influence does the story hold

Has it remembered to you some deed

And as at the birds you are pointing

Your young sons attention to draw

While he plays with toy cars laughing

What holds dear your attention in awe

It can't be the waters so placid

It can't be the birds of the air

For you've seen them before I know darling

Yet never did you show such care

The people around you are empty

And their faces I'm sure you don't see

So tell me Darling what holds you

So near yet so far from me

Then as you deeper doth enter

In the world of the book that you read

Come back and remember I love you

You're the strength of my days every need

Life Is A Dream In Reality

Life is a dream in reality
It brings to mind so many bygone days
It reaches out and touches hidden things
As it speeds time on its way
It plays with wants, wishes and desires
It seldom has one moment really dull
It is to me in all reality
A dream that lingers on and on
Why then do we waste our dream
In useless strife and quarrel
Why do we spend in frowns
Our sunshine years
We attain no heights in time
That time will not bring down
And we regret our wasted dream in tears
So let the Sun keep shining
In your heart today
And recall to memory once more
Those days of sun and flowers
Even tho they're on their way
To a place where greener pastures grow
It's easy to keep smiling

While the sun is shining bright
To laugh and love and sing and shout
Every moonlit night
Now try to brighten also
Your dreary side of life
And learn to love your sunless days as well
Then as your dreams linger on friend
You'll come to realize like me
That life is but a dream in reality
So smile and live on in your dreams

I've Searched and Searched

I've searched and searched but couldn't find
A written card with words of my mind
Verses which would truely say
How proud I am of this our day
The value which I place in you
And all the little things you do
That's why I hope you won't mind
These written cardless words of mine
For no one knew nor could they say
How much I love you every day

As The Sun Comes Up

As the Sun comes up I sometimes cry,
When I remember times long gone by
Times I spent so happy free
In my little home in the West Indies
The waters calm the air so warm
The Blue Caribbean with all its charm
The birds that sang in heavenly skies
These memories bring water to my eyes
The gold and silver Sunbeams fall
To brighten every bacchanal
The happy faces of boys and gals
Are Tropical memories I do recall
These sights I see bring back to me
Thoughts of my life so happy free
These bring me joy and happiness
For its back there I'll find my rest
The coral sands so clean and white
Calypso drums booming in the night
Tho its muscle straining works we do
Yet there we're happier friend than you
No race no creed can there put us down
'Cause this land it is all our own
No one can come from anywhere
To cause us racial problems here
So as I watch the Sun comes bright
Bringing day and giving light
So my heart in sorrow surely cries
As I long again for my Tropic Isles

I've Worked All Day For A Living

I've worked all day for a living
Lord I've worked so very long
Trying to earn my keeping
To keep me from doing wrong
It takes but want or hunger
It takes but pain or cold
To make a good man wander
From the narrow narrow road
So help me dear Lord help me
As I strive along my way
To live my working life for thee
Each night and every day
Give me strength each day to bear
The weight of this life's load
Hear and answer Lord my prayer
As I traverse this earthly road
And as my sunset draws near
And my noontime is all gone
Place then thy hand upon my arm
To help me move along
When life's eve has descended
From glory's throne you to me call
Forgive me for the wrongs I've done
Lift me from my deadly fall
Give me thy help and guidance
Teach me the right from wrong
Place on my lips full praise for thee
And in my heart your name in song

No Darn Business Of Yours

Brother — Sister — Father — Mother
Please listen to me
I didn't do it — You shouldn't say it
Just to bring heartaches to me
If my wife and I don't see eye to eye
That's no darn business of yours
If evil you think and evil do
Judge me not by works of you
Because I have no cause to stray
But should your gossip be sustained
It should still cause you no pain
Cause that's no darn business of yours
I never pry into your life
Please keep your gossip from my wife
Before you cause one to go away
And tho you may win for just a while
No parent will so easily lose a child
When 'twas no darn business of yours
You like the stories to spread about
From eye to ear from ear to mouth
But be careful fore you cross this man
Carry go bring come all right for you
But if it hurts me I'll sure fix you
Cause my wife my life and all my sorrow
Be they bright or be they dark
Be they old or new
There's just no way that its
Any darn business of yours

No Fault I Find In You

No fault I find in you
No cause to shout or curse
You dampen not my spirits
You make my life none worse
You take away no sorrows
You neither bring me pain
You speak not of bright tomorrows
You paint my death again
Yet in all your dullness
You have your reasons too
As you blank out all the sunshine
Which we enjoyed the whole day through
Yet tho your blanket circles
It serves o'er all
To enlighten our tomorrows
As we await them one and all
So darkness in your bleakness
A splendour you too do hold
It's one that brings the brightness
To the stars and moon of gold
It's one that lends our hearts throbs
To thoughts and plans of love
It's a splendour that elates us
To appreciate the world we love
It serves to bring to memory
Some reason for life again
As we look beyond you darkness
And re-evaluate our fellow-men

When Life Brings To Me Disgust

When life brings to me disgust

I stop and think of you

As dreary times doth harbour by

I stop and think of you

As evening brings the day to dusk

Or as sunrise brings the dawn

When I need the strength to go on

I stop and think of you

I think of you with all your pains

Since years and peoples passed

I think of how you always cared

Since years and peoples passed

I see your soft and greeny plains

Your warm blue, green and turquoise waves

I see your soft white coral sands

Where years and peoples passed

I think then of the years gone by

And wipe away my tears

I think of your peoples just like I

And wipe away my tears

So long in hurt and bitter pain

So peaceful, for so long to remain

Still waiting to be freed again

As I wipe away my tears

When I look up and see a star

I stop and think of you

When I recall homeland all you are

I stop and think of you

I think of all my hopes and plans

My coming back to you again

My warm and welcome Isle Cayman

Yes I stop and think of you

Look -- Look -- Look And See

Look — look — look and see
Listen to my every word
Hearken to my painful plea
'Tis not the only one you've heard
Ponder deep the things I say
Try your best to understand
That I think of you each day
You've won the heart of this poor man
I don't know or crave to hold
The answers to my questions deep
But each time to you I do behold
You at night doth haunt my sleep
You can't be to blame it's true
For the way that life evolves
And there's nothing you did do
So you can't now my problems solve
I know not if it's right or wrong
I care not what the world may say
I'll just try by verse song
To let you see things someday my way
Then maybe for a time I'll find
That which we all do search for
A time of joy a peace of mind

Filling this emptiness I abhor
Then when time has passed us by
And we look back in memories
I'll see you laughing tho I cry
Recalling when you stood by me
Alas alone tho then I'll live
I won't regret the price I pay
For to have known the love you give
Will keep me warm as yesterday

Iraq is like a 98 lb teenage girl who in a fit of rage
broke her younger sister's Kuwait arm
for stealing and spending all her savings and
while contemplating what to do for her sister
is set upon by a burly gang of motorcyclists
who held her hands, head and feet
to let their 250 lb Rambo-type leader America
rape her again and again as her preteen sisters
stand helplessly nearby with only nail files
and stones to throw at the raping gang members.

A Picture Of Life Has Started

A picture of life has started
In my eye now to appear
As Summers warmth is over
And Winter draweth near
As snows cold lips kiss mountains
Where Summers sun has shone
I see the love of heaven bright
At days end and each morn
I see the struggling leaves green
Turn gold or brown at a touch
Of the chilly breath of a cold breeze
Which now holds then in its clutch
The sun is shining yet tho
But ah alas 'tis only seen
For the cold Winters snowy blow
Makes its warmth become a dream
Yet here too one can vision
The reason why this must be
For the suns a heavenly protrusion
And Winters snow will earthly be
And men's hearts so like this land
Which Summers sun doth warm

Turns cold when temptation threatens
Forgetting Gods love so warm
Yes the seasons will all remind you
Of the way the world will change
But you fail to see you and me
As to each cycle we react so strange
We meet the Master warmly
When Spring is in the air
To grow hot for Him in Summer
When love and life is everywhere
But like the leaves of Autumn
We fade and wilt and fall
Soon as the cool sins winters breath
Doth to our hearts all call
But light a burning fire friend
Of Gods love deep in your heart
That the warmth of His Son
May shine on and on
And the cold of sins winter
Won't tear you apart

A Flower Is Lovely

A flower is lovely in bloom today
As bees take the honey it holds
Its fragrance fills you in some way
With fond memories of things you behold
However that flower 'twas just a bud
As protected it yesterday slept
Away from harm or dangers touch
But alas away from its true self
It lay in a bud which no one saw
The bees passed by it busily
The fragrance it held hidden lay
In a cloistered cell just yesterday
Then the time appeared and nature sang
The warmth of life its life began
To fill, until the bud burst apart
And joy of life filled all its heart
It tasted life as it could be
It saw the world huge happy free
It shared its beauty its fragrance too
It happily brought joy anew
Like this tiny flower in a bud asleep
Lies a little girl in her dreamlike haze
Hidden away while others weep
Searching for her in life's haze
'Til the warmth of life and love doth reach
And awaken the little one from her sleep
When her fragrance fills the earth with joy
She'll blossom to brighten the world of some boy

Darling Please Hold My Hand

Darling please hold my hand
And offer me your forgiveness
Darling let me be your man
And know again real happiness
Let me kiss your lips
See your face caress your fingertips
Darling let me let me love you

Let's you and I look for bright tomorrows
Darling please forget the bygone sorrows
Let me worship the one I adore
Hold me in your arms secure
Let me know that you will go
With me forever forever
And let me let me love you

Then Darling I'll be true to you
And by your side abide forever
There's no one who could replace you
As a precious pearl in this life of mine
I'm alone again in pain again
And my poor hearts aching for you
To touch you now to kiss your lips
And to caress your fingertips
Would be darling heaven for me
So Darling hold me and forgive me
But give me back the love I know
And Darling let me oh let me
Let me let me love you

If You'd Only Be A Wife

Sweetheart you say your love is gone
And that you no longer care for me
If you can answer these when I'm gone
Then I guess its best — I'll set you free
What you're gonna tell our son
When he is partly grown
And wants to know what happened to
The Dad he should-a known
And what you're gonna tell our boy
When he just can't understand
How a woman like you can go through life
With no heart for a loving man

So think it over sweetheart
Before you ruin now our life
I'll always be your husband
If you'd only be a wife
So think it over sweetheart
Don't spoil your young son's life
We could work it out together
If you'd only be a wife

I've tried everything my Darling
To win your love to me

Material things and Spiritual things
And dropping out from society
Could it be you're blinded now
By some past mistake that I've made
God knows I'm only Human
Don't you think to Him I've paid

I love you dear and need you so
I hoped you'd understand
That the clumsy methods that I used
Were to try to bring you to your man
Most women if they care at all
For any man they've known
Would have fought against any broad
Who threatened to wreck her home

No other woman ever really could
Have broken us apart
So why don't you drop your ego
And listen to your heart
I once tried to make you jealous, yes
In the hope you would cling to me
But you've turned it to a weapon dear
With which to fight and torture me

How'd You Like To Be

How'd you like to be a Human traffic Island

And stand as trucks and cars go by

Silently giving to them directions

Hoping that they all do you spy

Watching as they take and follow

Each command your hand doth give

Wondering if one but swerves or lingers

If they'd stop and let you live

How'd you like to be a Human Ferry

Being daily laden with heavy cars

Tossing waters off your polished bows

Fearing the sea which cradles you with love

Wondering which wave will pull you down

And throughout how many storms you'll live

How'd you like to be a Human auto car

Taking lots of peoples far away

Touching speeds that lift you off the ground

Or going slowly chugging up the hill

Governed by that foot upon your gas lifeline

Wondering how many accidents'll pass and let you live

How'd you like to be a Human Aeroplane

Flying far far across distant skies

Taking hundreds in your tight embrace

Caressing each with singing engines drone

Wondering of the flight that'll bring you down

Wondering if you'll land safe and live

How'd you like to be a Human Being

A thing that has a free will and might

A machine that can within itself reason

A differentiate between wrong and right

A being that has power to take or give

A conscience heart and life within itself

This you are and this you can remain

If only you are not afraid to live

Why Do You Descend So Bleak

Why do you descend so bleak
Hiding the world around
Letting us have false lights to seek
To move from town to town
You're the master of the other world
Where shadows and lights ne'er go
You're the cover wherever evil is found
You're the cause of much grief and woe
Darkness —— why must I speak of you
In such a dreary way
What purposes you in garb so meek
To stumble us each day
Why rejoice you at our downfall
And ne'er a helping hand lend
How can you hold hatred now for all
So deep, when you we did not offend
Before our earth was opened
We're told you shrouded it round
But at Gods loving light it happened
That your power was cast down
It seems e'er since you've wondered
How with our God to even the score
But alas Darkness tho you've pondered
His light will overpower you evermore
And that king of yours the Devil
Will try souls in your clutches to pull
But God saves all from evil
So your domain 'twill ne'er be full

Today Is April The Twenty Fourth

Today is April the twenty fourth
My poor hearts crying for all its worth
And what's the reason? I'll tell you
Tho it concerns the girl that I love true
She touched my head, my hand and my heart
Then showed me the plane on which she shall depart
I longed I locked I prayed whilst she did the same
Whispering "I love you" and calling each other by name
Then inside I could see she started to weep
There were tears in her eyes tears on her cheeks
She pressed close to me once more where I stood
Repeating a promise to love and wait if I would
I gave her my answer quite broken and dry
But I had to to keep her from seeing me cry
As I held her close realizing 'twas time to part
I felt her tremble and shudder as my heart fell apart
I looked in her eyes there clearly I could see
All the true love and trust she had for me
And I was glad and proud then as even now I am
That I'd been lucky to find her in Cayman
I'll keep visions of yesteryear right through the years
But deep in my heart there'll be no fear
For by the words spoken whilst walking the sands
I know she loves me and my Isle, my native Cayman
Her Mom is too wonderful for me to speak of fully now
Else I could continue till I've a deep wrinkled brow
Still for the time I'd spend to be to her just
I'd only be able to say
"Thanks for your Respect and your Trust"

The Fall Of Snowflakes

Just across these cool cool waters
There are mountains, rivers, trees
With hard cold frozen waters
In the Ice capped blue Rockies
On their icy side still lingers
Visions of the summer past
Where we played in games of laughter
'Till the Autumn chilled us fast
Now the clouds all lazily flutter
And the birds all southwards fly
As the moving brook stills mutters
Which we heard in days gone by
Down the sleek and polished ski-ways
Glide the skiers one by one (everyone)
Playing on those snowy highways
Day and night they go on and on
Looking with laugh filled wonder
At the demon cold and white
As each ski-lift takes them yonder
To some new and dizzying (distant) height
Yes down they go on the mountain
Floating freely o'er frozen ground
Enjoying the thrill of Winter's morning

Listening deep to that silent sound
It is ('Tis) but the fall of snowflakes
Soft upon the ground so white
Like the cloak of some great angel
Falling o'er the dark of night
Oh so soft yet so destructive
Oh so light yet bares such weight
That when as glaciers — its objective
Seems but one of death and hate
On the highways and the hill roads
Drifts were formed by Winters wind
But they've hardened into icy ghouls
To restrict our kith and kin
Oh soft snowflake softly falling
Light on yonder mountainside
What tomorrow pray be your calling
How much sorrow must we abide
Rocky mountains, trees and rivers
Covered by the snow white cap
Keep warm your head cover your shoulders
Soon spring will bring the warm sun back

Oh What A Way To Live My Life

Oh what a way to live my life

Oh what a pain in my memories

Oh what a joy gone I used to know

Before this when my life 'twas happy free

When life was simple warm and true

When I in thoughts and mind lived a younger life

When problems of this world so cruel huge

Did not enter in to destroy my mind

But past is past and gone is gone

Sad, wishes ne'er can come back true

The realities of this world goes on

The hardships and the aching sorrows too

Yet in my sub and distant thoughts

I see again that life I've lost

I dream anew my thoughts of old

I think of lands where I belonged

I wonder at the dreams that are

I labour in their ways of life

No recompense will I ever find

To ease these pains of mind and life

Now as I sit in half repose

I gaze again at this life I know

I see the year as it swiftly goes

Unable to stay awhile more with me

And so in lonely solitude

I must recall those slower days

When my heart 'twas light and beautiful

And my mind 'twas ne'er in this foggy haze

That's why I sigh thinking of my life

That's why I ponder if it's right

That's why I've strength to travel on

To try again and pay life's price

Oh what a way to live

Oh is it is it right

The John's Graffiti

We are the John's Graffiti
And being you're well read
We hope you will fill us in
With wisdom words instead
"I come from a long line of stinkers"
"See we give the same relief to all
rich or poor, male or female"
The painters work was all in vain
The — house poet strikes again,
Truly the seat of wisdom, equality and understanding
Be friendly speak to your next door neighbour
Long as the door is open you're
welcome to come sit awhile,
Don't blame me for the words of wit
I'm only here to collect it
Ring a bell or pull a rope
Here in true solitude find hope
Here castles are built and fortresses fall
So keep us informed from every new wall
Each day as you sit reading what's new
Fill us in with the latest we're curious too
The poets work will be in vain
Once the crappy painter strikes again

When by you completed
This book of wisdom and of wit
Will e'er fondly remind you
Of where you once did sit
Quite unique will it be
No two just quite the same
Your own collections of writings
By the best in the game
Each tidbit that you enter
Will make this your very own
A tribute to the Walls Arts
The oldest expressions the world has ever known

We all must do that in life
which we think is right
even tho we know it may not be right
and pay the consequences
for our actions.

Hey Little Girl Tripping

Hey little girl tripping through the grass

What do you ponder deep

With head bent downwards so steadfast

As a hand your chin upkeeps

Has life been bitter in your youth

To cause you grief and woe

Or have you stumbled on some truth

Which you'd rather never know

Or then again perhaps you see

In the clouds or in the sky

A call back of a past memory

Which brings tears to your eye

Now even tho the time is short

And life is so unsure

You still can play some useful part

If life you will endure

So as the warm sun shineth clear

Upon your long hair fair

Put on your face a smile my dear

Let's travel on somewhere

Let's go to places unforeknown

To you or even I

To heights unreached, depths unsearched

To extremes which passed us by

Let's live and love and laugh and sing

Let's walk and run and play

Let's enjoy now Earth's everything

And be fulfilled today

Then as the evening settles down

And calls us to repose

We'll go content without a frown

To that future we did chose

Life Is An Empty Place To Be

When one's alone
Life holds nothing at all for me
When I'm alone
Nothing that comes can ever bring
The sunshine and warmth of the Spring
That fills my soul my everything
If I'm not alone
Love means pain and promises heard
Now I'm alone
Love to me is a four letter word
Since I'm alone
Love is a happy girl and boy
Sharing together their trouble and joy
But these ecstasies I no longer enjoy
'Cause I'm alone
You were to me full happiness
Afore I was alone
You thrilled me with your tenderness
When you were my own
You gave me reason to love and live
A pleasure to work and of myself give
To be able to know we could then live
Never alone

So give back to me the world I knew
Don't leave me alone
Give this poor fool one chance with you
I won't leave you alone
Forgive the wrongs I might have done
Come back and be my only one
Let me be warmed by love of your Sun
Then I won't be alone

Just Another Mock Trial

This is not my first trial
For you've tried me oft before
I saw your recollections
E'en as I crossed the floor
I've seen you sit in judgment
On me even as right now
I know your preconceivement
Of justice yet to come
I've stood before on trial
At long distant courts and lands
Watched faultless condemnation
Of which you washed your hands
Yet deep within your chambers
'Twas you who guilt did lie
Square on my guiltless shoulders

The waiting crowd to pacify
I've stood on Afric's seashore
With friendly outstretched hand
Which you did grasp and shackle
Why I did not understand
'Til in your deep summation
'Tis better them you said
To work our fields and Indies
Than the weakling Indian red
For of them here it seemeth
That alas there be no end
This your justice given to me
To me who came as friend
I've stood in wide arena
Heard Death himself walk by
Heard loud the cry for blood
Of the lions who would try
Then waiting for your signal
The gates of freedom shut
Your final worded decision
To let my sure death out
I've been to sea for ages
Watched man die and suffer deep
'Til its torture cracked my awakeness
Foul dreams wrecked all my sleep

Saw plants for king and country
Given water which man craved
Whilst the thirsty dying soul
You sent to a watery grave
I arose to fight for freedom
To clear my name in life
I stood firm to hold my freedom
To stand for the others rights
I fought the lion charging
Tore wide its jaws apart
I gave up my home and country
A free life for few to start
Yes I have stood on trial
Before Sir such as you
Each time as man unequal
Each time condemned untrue
Yet thru all I search for
The place the time the year
But once justice to see given
To one such as standeth here
For thru ages past before me
And for lifetimes yet to come
I'll seek that goal forever
Father to son, to son, to son

Today On The Waters I Sailed

Today on the waters I sailed on a ship
My thoughts and my dreams were far off
My memory wandered to some Islands tip
Where beautiful days I'd spent oft
My heartaches and sorrows I then did not know
Nor was I concerned with life
My best was to love and to let love grow
My mind never seeketh for strife
Now alas I have wandered so far away
From those beautiful days I did know
I've lost all my true friends
And also my ways
To a lost soul-like existence did go
My memory wonders, my aching heart cries
My dreams they all just linger still
I wish I'd not listened to all of those lies
Which corrupted me and changed my will
My will was to live on so innocently
And enjoy all that God did bestow
But no longer does Peace or Joy follow me
I've lost all happiness I did know
And alas I cry in my heart to be free
Today on the waters I sailed on a ship
My dreams and my thoughts were far off
My memory wandered to my Islands tip
And I longed, yes, I longed to be HOME

Why Do You Blanket Me

Why do you blanket me around
In your grey and dismal shroud
Why do you block out the views
Of which we are so proud
Why do you cause such dronings
Of the horn upon this ship
Why do you listen ten'tively
For bells ringing every trip
Where do you come from cloudlike
What is your purpose pray
Why do you hang so ghostlike
O'er road — and sea— and bay
You silent touchless creature
You damage causing fiend
Why don't you lift your drooping head
And float away somewhere
You're as light as drifting clouds yes
You're as grey as night at dusk
You're penetrable yet envelope
Like a smoky cloud of dust
You plague our journeys over
You harass our sailings back
You're the cause of highway sorrows
You cause havoc on many a track
But yet somehow you serve too
I guess in your own way
To show us life's bright side
For fog when you lift your blanket
We still sail the Fogless tide

How Old Are You

How old are you how brave are you

How long have you travelled this way

How much do you know where do you go

On your endless journeys each day

Have you learned or taught the language

Which you whisper to the reef

Does the sands upon the shoreline

Your countless secrets keep

When you're mad with white teeth gleaming

Is your anger from within

And when you're calm and peaceful

Are you then at peace with men

While the ship doth sail upon you

Do you hold her up with scorn

Or is this a compliment good and true

One for which you first were born

And far below your deep embrace

How does your salt mines last

To keep you so salty sweet

Today as throughout the past

Can you speak and tell me truly

While your journeys without end

Has taken you completely

To all the hidden haunts of men

That within your enchanting bosom

If a heart or conscience lives

There are no regrets of destruction

Such as you sometimes gives

And then again dear Tide and Sea

You're still my constant friend

Your love and warmth 'tis part of me

From birth until my end

It Really Is A Wonder

It really is a wonder

That ships sail on the seas

When waves as big as houses

Grow taller yet than trees

Where waters all combine

To mountain size they grow

And turn and toss upon it

The ships which o'er it go

At ten at twelve or twenty

Knots they labour on

Whilst hundred knot winds

Slam the gushing seas along

On the top just like a toothpick

Which in an auto washer floats

These ships are tossed and tumbled

Large tankers, ships and boats

Again at times the fog falls

To blanket all around

To deaden silence hamper

Broken only as horns sound

Or else the rain is sheeting

The snow and hail and Sun

To wet to chill to pound to burn
These stalwart ships each one
Yet on these small bits wander
Just like man upon this earth
So small and so insignificant
Yet they encompass all its girth
A searching light —— a moving mind
A prop or sail that's filled
Man goes on to the higher things
Like ships, at each port to be filled
The dark and dismal clouds above
So solemnly look down
Upon the small and listing ship
Which lumbers on and on
It really is a wonder
That wood steel and concrete all
Floats o'er each wave that tries so hard
Yet seldom 'neath one falls
It really is a wonder
That these ships on seas exist
And maybe it's that danger which
No true Seaman can resist

What Is Right Or Wrong

What is right or wrong you ponder
What is good, bad or unjust
What is fair and even treatment
For and from those that you trust
Should life remain full bitter
When a spread of joy you hold
Because you think and vainly titter
Of what the future it may hold
But suppose in lifes short journey
You mayhap doth meet a friend
Whom you'd like to share your journey
With as you travel on again
But alas as often befalls
You do wait too long instead
Of answering when your heart calls
And when you do — your friend is dead
Then you spend your every moment
In regret of what was right
For you've lost your precious moment
For a few hours or days so bright
Then as you travel onwards
Soon you come to find at last
What you thought was so wrong once

Is but mere steps along lifes pass
Then too late you'll hope to recall
The moments you could have shared
When someone offered you their all
But you refused 'cause this you feared
What is right or wrong you ponder
As time and life doth pass you by
Take life —— live it with its love and wonder
Too soon you too may have to pass it by

Remember the words of the ancient Slaves;
Laugh not at the old or inflicted
for you may one day share their plight
but rather laugh at the young and the lively
for in their ignorance they are wasting
that which you can never again in life achieve

Speaking of Love

There are those who at times in life
doth sit and gaze in awe,
at the wonderment of all the life
they've lived yet never saw
The life as human beings all, as women or men too,
as those in love as those loved
by a warm true being like you

Forgetful of the times they lay in brokenhearted fear,
Content it seems to spend a new a new yet wasted day
Never caring for the heights
it seems that they can never reach,
the heights where on they too may know
Love Joy and contented Bliss

Speaking of Love to these cold hearts
doth bring it seems but pain
for all the love that's to them given,
'twill be it seems all vain
Aloof and far Cold and above beyond and out of grasp
These hearts do look with bitterness
or in deceitful scorn they laugh

But do not Love be fast to judge
and do not their ways condemn
They too like you did one time
trust in like ways of other men
Their hearts and souls did one time
swell in pride in love and warmth
they too like you did one time
seek the peace they now have lost

One time a lone and lonely heart
did swell in joy and light,
One time, now gone, they saw within
each new day hopes so bright
That lone and long and lonely road
on which they too have trod,
did serve to lead them further yet
from life from love from God

Yet Love or Friend as you can see,
there rested once within
some good some hope some longing
for all that they knoweth not
Oh Friend so now enclosed are they
in sorrow in shame apart alone unfree
they too have lost along lifes long road
I know they've walked that road with me

In This Wacky Wacky City

In this wacky wacky city
Where I did one time stray
I chanced to meet deceitfulness
So oft upon the way
I had to take a second look
Around for what I'd need
Then days of childhood past came back
As the answer to this breed
So now the old and aged one
Whom I have so long known
Has stood to now be my helper
Even tho I now move on
So he has touched you briefly
And he to you will teach
You never should have crossed me
In works or plans or speech
I give to you my friend here
Dr Do Good warm and true
He'll give to you your well deserved
He'll give to you your due
And as you think of me in time
You bigot fiend or bitch
You will recall my doctor friend
As you itch and itch and itch

The BC's SC Shaft

Social Credit is my master
It's useless to voice my wants
They maketh me to lie down in
Green pastures for
They forecloseth my home
Yea they repossesseth my car
Their finance rebuilding policies
Crippleth me
Yea tho I go deeper and deeper in debt
I get no answer to my pleas
For only a poor bleeding taxpayer am I
They prepare and eat their feast before me
They renew my knowledge of hunger
They renege on small advances we'd made
While the NDP we were under
Our education medicine and welfare
They dike back or dam over
With shovels and finger we stand meek
To stop up any overflow or leak
Now tho I walk miles to work
I need fear no evil
For I no longer have anything of value
My standard of living has gone under
Surely rising taxes and cutbacks shall follow
The rest of their term
And by then I shall be in the poorhouse
Of want forever

Daily Prayer

Our premier

Which art in Victoria

Billy be thy name

Thy vindictiveness come

Thy will must be done

On Conservatives and Liberals

As it is on NDP-ers

Give us this day our

Daily bread and water

And forgive us for asking

For basic necessities and rights

As we must realize these belong

Only to the rich business peoples

Send us with our picks and shovels

As you deliver us from equality

And socialism

For thine was the election

By big business bought to give you glory

Assuring a fast return to the fifties

Once again to see the poor shafted

Forever and ever

Amen

These Prison Bars May Bind Me

These prison bars may bind me,
These chains may hold my feet,
These cuffs upon my wrist may welters grow,
These walls may cut my freedom,
These guards may stop my moves,
But this prison is helpless 'gainst my soul

For my souls-a-burning fire
burning deep deep down within of me
Yes my souls a living fire
And my Jesus is looking (after) out for (me)

These courts have passed a sentence
On the falsehoods they did hear
These laws have stood content me to condemn
These peoples laugh so scornful
Because they've cut me down
They don't know in my soul I'll rise again

So you cold and cruel prison wall
I have no fear of you,
Altho my better self you'll try to break
For within me there's assurance of
a better life to which I go
And when you've killed me — my soul
my God shall take

A Crow On A Log

A crow on a log
With feathers ruffled slight
As cool mountain air blows upon
Those feathers black as night
A few short hours
Stops for relief
Then to the air takes wing
For four or five hundred feet
To perch softly by that spring
And even as the crow departs
A multicoloured pigeon
Arrives to gaze in wonder awe
Then wiggle off soft cooing
Down to the water's edge he goes
A Seagull thereby he joins
To seek on the receding tide
Such food as they might find
No company says he needs I
And thus with white wings spreading
The Seagull lifts itself on high
Straight bound it seems to heaven
Then stop I for a lasting glance
To drink in the music sweet
Which flows from trees above my head
Where red-breasted robins tweet
The birds abound at Summertime
Here on the beach and sand
It seems contented they remain
To show beauty simple unto man

And Near Near Evermore

Autumns days are over
Nights cold on us falls
Need I again to wish for
Evenings warming powers
Winter may fall o'er us
So softly creeps the cold
Yet in memories warm I'll be
If your face therein I hold
Another night now ending
A new days dawns begun
Wherein I'll wait full hoping
To see you 'fore set of Sun
A new nighttime eternal
Or so to me it seems
Yet even therein I'm happy
As you haunt all of my dreams
And so my friend tho passing
We are like shadows on a floor
I'll wait to one day be again
Around near near evermore

I Saw Three Fishing Boats

I saw three fishing boats
Three fishing boats
Three fishing boats at sea
Just off the bow, the starboard side
The end of a huge ferry
Their wake like silver ribbons lay
Six paths across the waves
Reflecting the blue hue of the skies
As they went upon their ways

I saw three fishing boats at sea
One trawler led the pack
One shrimper followed close behind
One gill netter at the back
I saw three fishing boats at sea
Move carelessly along
Their thoughts rest on their fishing trips
As they lazily moved along

I looked and saw three fishing boats
Their white sails all a-shiny
Go moving o'er the salty brine
So gracefully so silently
The crews all gazed laughingly
They waved their hands in glee
As friendship it reached out
Across the morning sea

I saw three boats
Three fishing boats
Three times in unison
Then with our speed
And urgency

We passed by and were gone
Three times three boats
I watch pass by
As at my work I toiled
My body here mechanically
My heart with them awhile

Three times I looked so wishfully
Then like the fox and grapes
Concluded as we passed them by
As they tossed high in our wake
Oh surely tho they happy seem
To laze there on silent sea
With all the tossing we they give
How seasick they must be

So with that consolation I
Returned hard to my toil
With but the painted picture yet
Fresh in my mind awhile
A picture of three times three ships
Their wakes like ribbons silver
Which moved so gracefully along
While noisily-by we lumbered
Three times three boats
Three fishing boats
Some sail some motor powered
Three times three boats
Three fishing boats
Brings back memories remembered

Cold Dark And Dismal Grey

Cold dark and dismal grey

The world in silence lies

The Sun no longer warms the day

Nor brightens Summer's skies

The birds to nest have taken wing

The trees wet bend their heads

As Autumn's cold and wintry touch

Falls overall instead

The rain makes puddles on the ground

The leaves start all to change

The feel of winters majesty

Their colours rearrange

The old school bell is clanking

As the Summer break is o'er

The laughing screaming playing kids

Now hard o'er their books pore

The long and bright Summer's eve

Gives way so soon it seems

To Autumns shortening of days

To fit in with nature's scheme

We look at lawns green uncut

Which now no longer grow

As they too wait so solemnly

For first fall of Winters snow

But thru it all there remains

The hope of coming Spring

The clearing skies the shining moon

New buds grass and everything

Tho cold and dark and dismal grey

Now the world in silence lies

We'll take our rest and wait awhile

For tomorrows Summer skies

I Have Leaned Against The Bough

I have leaned against the bough

And long silent called your name

I have watched the songbird's flight

Singing loudly e'er the same

I have seen the setting sun

Your cheeks try to imitate

I have felt the summer's wind

Warm as voice when you spake

I have listened to a babe

Cry softly out in laughter

And from it all I still recall

The vision lasting after

For still you stay the vision

Who precedes each lovely dream

Still you stay the face I see

When life's passed away it seems

Still you reach into the realm

Of deep secret distant thought

Still you in dreamlike imagery

Stay there throughout it all

So I will lean against the oak

And 'gain softly call to you

I will whisper on the wind

Long as my life's not through

I will look into the skies

To recall eyes set in your face

A shining brilliance ever there

Which time cannot erase

Then as I lean against the oak

I'll softly call thy name

I will lean before the wind

Like sailing ship of fame

I will lean towards thy call

Each time the soft wind chimes

I lean, I lean towards thy call

Until the end of time

November 6, 1982

She Smiled And Smiled

She smiled and smiled again
'most to herself it seemed
Then marvelled at the picture
She as a child had seen
Then she reached out her wizened hand
To grasp and hold his tight
The years had passed but everyone
The time was always right
Somehow, somewhere,
Some reason unbeknown
She thought only of the many years
She was loved by and loved him
Both hair of angel white whisps
Around enveloped full their face
As into her eyes his thought migrated
And back thru his he hers appreciated
Such light of love she touched him
A frail in age they struggled yet
Their only help in age of time
Each the other soundlessly communicated
And love came back to them assist
Two who the years had seen full
Two in each other understood

Then now and always would
Her wrinkled hands grasped onto his
His knarled bent fingers held
And caused a bond again to be
Their shared silent understanding
So many years past sixty now
Part eighty and even ninety
Their help the other did expect
And need not of outside pity
She smiled and did again
As so many years and years
Lent to him her supportive love
Her strength his ever needed
The years had wizened both
Yet never dimmed her eye's light
As his sparkled back as bright
Each so still in remembrance forever

~~~~~~~~~~~~~~~~~~~~~~~~~~~~

Note: Written on November 4, 2012 - we were in the China Kitchen in Maple Ridge, and an elderly couple were sitting behind us. He was much older than she, and very frail. She had finished her supper, but he was a very slow eater. She waited patiently, watching the aquarium fish, and commented to him about it.

If I Should Die Tomorrow

If I should die tomorrow

I wonder where you'd be

Would you take time off from work

Would you remember me

My life, my heart, my hopes, my dreams

Would be all at their end

Would you think back at me as man

Would you think back of me as friend

My left behinds all in your hands

To steward out would go

How fair and full would you decide

Where each thing it would go

And when a voice calls out at night

From deep apart to ask

For help or love or just advice

Would you be up to the task

I wonder if tonight I die

What to you I have been

Would fair and even be your hand

Please keep them all as friends

24-04-07

With Scornful Eyes

With scornful eyes you upon me gaze
With look of dark condemnation
Your eyes so like a minister's it seems
Gazing hell fire e'er o'er your congregation
You feel that my style of life is wrong
And long it seems to put it to an end
You'd love to openly me condemn
But fear-filled you hold it back in
For you in all your Godliness
You in all your righteous self-reproach
You in all your holier than thou
Sit there alas afraid of me now
You with your disapproving glance
Which traverse from my feet to head
Which with nary a word me yet condemn
You sit there so silently instead
Your glances are reflected 'mongst you three
Your eyes visions of your inner mind-speak
Your heart's thoughts are revealed to me
As I sit by to feed your disbelief
You wonder if these offsprings are all mine
Then surely wives two must mine be
So thinking you would me like to be

You Are And I Am Not

You are and I am not -- single

I am and you are not -- married

If I was you wouldn't be -- single

Yet if you weren't and I wasn't -- single/married?

You would be and I wouldn't be -- married

But unless I become -- single

Or until you become -- married

Or both of us cease as we are

You will remain -- single

I will hope to remain -- married

Tho if we both could change

That you could be -- married

What you are not

And I could become -- single

What you are now

Then I would change you

Into what I am now -- married

And after changing myself

Into what you are now -- single

I would then revert back

To what I am now -- married

That you would be and I would be also -- married

I Am Sure You Can't Imagine

I am sure you can't imagine
It's simple as can be
The place is rather private
The players he and she
She whispers "will it hurt"
"Of course not" he replies
"It's a very simple process
Lay back and close your eyes"
"It's getting rather painful"
As tears came to her eyes
"It's hurting something awful
It must be quite a sin"
"Calm yourself my Darling
Open wide so I can get more in"
Suddenly with a little shout
"Now that it's all over" he slowly pulls it out
Now that you've read this poem
A dentist is what you'd find
It's not what you were thinking
You've just got a dirty mind

Oh My Children How I Wish

Oh my children how I wish the time
The time of your youth it hadn't passed so fast
Oh my children how I wish the time
The time of your youth it hadn't passed so fast
I sat today and looked upon
A child five months of age
With thoughts deep thoughts of children
My own now old of age
Of years I'd spent aworking just
Our sustenance to make
Without a thought to passing time
And the toll that time would take
I've never now it seems to me
Spent time my young ones with
Time just to coo and love and laugh
Watch their eyes sparkle yet from it
I've never taken time to stay
After their steps were taken
To marvel at their own belief
That one more would yet uphold them
I've never now it seems had time
To play the games they cared
To spend an hour or a week
Where we could each other share

I've never had it seems the time
Save to work and work and worry
What little time on them I spent
Seems 'twas always in a hurry
They grew, I've grown and time has passed
So fast they now seems lost
It's all because I've always worked
Unrealizing of the cost
Oh my children how I wish the time
The time it hadn't passed
How I'd like to recall the years
Let each tender moment last
Oh my children how I wish that I
Could watch you coo and cry
Could watch the spit bubbles roll
Off your pursed lips in smiled reply
Could sit and feel you wet my knee
Or spill food my shirt upon
Could waken to feed you at night
Hold you close while storms roll on
Oh how I wish I could teach
You one step alone to take
Or mend a broken dolly's arm
Take you fishing at the lake

Show you things for the first time
See them new thru your bright eyes
Watch you learn to run learn to swim
Learn to balance a bike and ride
Oh how I wish the time we had
Hadn't passed so swiftly by
That we could start anew again
Now I haven't so hard to try
I'd love now that my works secure
And the nest we have is safe
To recall all our past put offs
And fulfill them each today
Oh my children how I wish the time
The time it hadn't passed
That I could hold you young and small
Listen to your baby laugh
Feel your heart beat against my arms
As you snuggled tiny there
With tiny dimpled bootied feet
And head yet scarce of hair
Oh my children how I wish the time
The time it hadn't so fast passed
And I could recall in actuality
All our tender memories past

But since all I can now do
Is recall in thought the time
It's best I think that you share
At least these thoughts of mine
Then mayhaps as you older grow
And life calls you like I
You'll see the beauty of the time
Before it passes by
Mayhap you'll stop to smell a rose
Or hold an infant's hand
Or watch a caterpillar crawl
Some dead limb or muddy sand
Fly some kite take a sunny hike
Or sit watching the seas just lap
'Gainst secluded salty quiet shores
As some newborn baby naps
Feels fingers small yours held within
Give grasp of fearless trust
Then maybe you will not have missed
What I now feel was missed by us.
Oh my children how I wish the time
The time of your youth it hadn't passed so fast
Oh my children how I wish the time
The time of your youth it hadn't passed so fast

I Walk The Empty Beach

'Tis daybreak -- I walk the empty beach
I scan the wet and mossy rocks
Strewn o'er the waste of sand
And I alone -- I -- here alone
No Friday's barefoot print I find
To trace in haste for vocalizing
Unknowing that on finding
Both mute and blind may be
The one whose footprints are not here
But for whose prints I scan
As I walk the empty beach

I pause awhile and listen
Listen to the murmur of the tide
A low low lapping music melody
Which falls upon my ears
Whispering my quest to pursue
For lone, alone am I
Here on this empty beach
While day is yet its eyes
Struggling to force open
Amid the obscuring grey clouds
Which blinds its blinking eye
As I walk this empty beach

But hark now there awhile
I hear the cawing of a crow
The whistle of a seagull
The chirping of a meadowlark
Joining in the lap tides choir
To realize me that I am not alone
No Friday's footstep bare and scant
Mark this the fresh tide washed sand
No human voice I hear nor see
But yet I know I'm not alone
As crabs crawl nearby silent
So cautiousless they frighten
The lone lost human walking
The empty seeming beach

Birds cascade and serenade
Bees sing soft just out of reach
All too seeking their Friday's print
Someplace as along alone they go
But unlike me know they're not alone
As we share the empty beach

Glance Up You Auto Driver

Glance up you auto driver
In your mirror back to see
Swift auto coming towards you
Closing space so urgently
Nearer yet yet never slacking
'Til his number you can read
Then so close his reversed number
Is by you no longer seen
Pull you off on highways shoulder
Just to let this speeder by
But he swerves and laughs so loudly
Slows to a crawl as cars speed by
Back upon the legal roadway
Once again at legal speed
Swerving o'er the lines full painted
In your mirror watch him weave
Ah you think he is behind me
Again relax in peace can I
Yet once more the distance narrows
On should right he drives besides
Turn your head to right watch him
Face beet red eyes half closed
Nodding nodding ever nodding

Trying hard to fight repose
Smirk upon his face is written
By the artist alcohol
As he waves a limp right hand
Causing him to lose control
Fast into your lane it sends him
You swerve fast him to avoid
As he shows his bottled left hand
While his car with yours collide
Sharp into your right front fender
Spinning you 'round and away
Your control now wrenched from you
He pushes you off the highway
Fast your speed had been tho legal
Fast the rocks and trees pass by
While sideways at forty fifty
Into deep dug ditch you fly
Breaking glass crash about you
Metal tearing screams in pain
Rubber pleads for better traction
Gas fumes fills your breathing air
Belted fast into your seat you
Sit there pinned back by the wheel
Two arms limp hang o'er the column

No pain sensation do you feel
Down your face blood flows like liquid
O'er your mouth to your left cheek
On your right is his torn bumper
Which rests hard against your cheek
At last it's raining oh so welcome
Cooling heat you feel it seems
'Til the rain send out its fragrance
It's not rain it's gasoline
Sprinkle, shower, drizzle drip, drip
For what seems eternity
You can see him in his car still
In drunken stupor injury free
Watch as he retrieves his bottle
Takes one last long drink and then
Looks at you and smiling waves you
Unaware of the pain you're in
Then in hopeful helpful gesture
He to you a cigarette shows
Takes your silence for affirmative
Oblivious to the threat it'll pose
Caring not for gas which lingers
Like a blanket everywhere
He intent to share his 'bacco

Strikes a match into the air
For another seeming lifetime
Like the seconds past that's flown
You relive your life so quickly
'Til by explosions you are torn
Fast and furious hot and scorching
You can feel the flames engulf
'Til you watch your body perish
And silently cry out 'enough'
Glance up you new auto driver
In your mirror back to see
Swerving auto coming towards you
Closing space so urgently
Nearer yet yet never slacking
'Til his number you can read
It's but another drunken driver
Murder itself there at that wheel
He speeds He slows
He swings He swerves
He crosses lane and line
He tails He trails
He hails He fails
To observe the rules each time

The Bloodhounds

They trudged and fell and injured were
Yet they may have been saved they say
Had human hand but got to them
But the bloodhounds were on holiday

Eight years in youth companion with
A child in mind tho twenty-eight
Lost for a week in lake or trees
These searchers sought till late

But when they tried to help enlist
From the hounds who follow blood
On holiday from work they were
These high trained essential cur

On yonder mountain daily fed
They frolicked and they played
While child and man-child perished they
As if no one really cared

Now back again in kennel safe
Their toil once more to endure
Sleep eat and wait for urgent call
On lake or land or shore

Still calls comes scarce this hamlet to
For the use of such as these
The bloodhounds who on holidays were
When lost two youths did freeze

'Twas summer time among the hills
Where hot and dry the wind did blow
The dusty streets with litter parched
The mountains tall with unmelting snow

The beauty of nature full displayed
On lake and hill and tree
O'ershadowed by nature's ugliness
The poor the afflicted the unfree

Mankind in excess he had cast
On side of road beach and street
The bottles, boxes and the cans
Wherefrom conveniently he did eat

And from these cast off garbage bits
To eek a living out they tried
These youths one aged by still a child
Held back he slight in mind

Tho work he sought oft was refused
For nature made his back unstraight
So from the shoulders stooped he down
Tho moving on in lively gait

Still often times he could be seen
With such little as he had
Share with the hungry boy or girl
Share with the bird the dog or cat

And summer came as oft before
So along his ways he trudged
To collect the discarded empty things
Which brought pennies he to for food

Up ditch down ditch 'long seashore
By road or street they walked
In happy childlike chatter they
Thru the dust and bushes sought

A sack across their shoulders lay
Each with their days rewards
Of cans and bottles they had found
For the refunds they would afford

Then tripping lightly as so oft
Along the creek bank high were they
Yet something dreadful happened there
Which still we wonder of today

Did nature see to short their time
To rest their pains their toils their fears
To give succour to those suffering
By shouting out their earthly years

Or was it hand of man that moved
Their agony short to make
Or merely slip of once sure foot
On rocky path they'd so oft take

No one will know or e'er reveal
What plight 'twas theirs by fate
For when their bodies they were found
Life to save, it was too late

For silent lake stood silent by
While the river screamed in pain
As the whispered cries across the creek
O'er and o'er called out their names

Still but few can read nature's sounds
When upon the winds it blows
Save the birds wild the trained hounds
And the beasts which in forests grow

So as man toiled and prayers were sent
Their prayers and works were lost
For the help they needed never came
Making their lives the final cost

Now around one hears the mourning town
Cry shame upon the holidays
Which were granted to the rescue bloodhounds
Frolicking unrecalled thru those fatal days

And On

And on they ride and ride and on they ride
Going ever round and round
'Til the wheels have left a weathered track
Into its hardwood ground
The thrills and laughter still peals out
The smiles light up small faces
As each believes a driver true
This electrical twirl has made 'em
And watch the cycles and the boats
Each the same on different seating
Each but the whirl of just one wheel
Running 'gain o'er new ground seeming
And up above the same wheel turns
To thrill the yet much older
Yet 'tis but the self-same twirly wheel
Which propelled the tots in wonder
Yet each new year it reappears
With full as much anticipation
To thrill the every young at heart
Who rejuvenate again its action
And on

Some Fancy University

For 'less you've been to SFU

To them you have no brains

I've never been to SFU

But I'm happier just the same

So I'm looked on with disdain

By some professional students who

Would envy e'er my gains

For 'less you've been to SFU

To them you have no brains

I've never been to SFU

But I'm happier just the same

As an autodidact I've learnt and been

Thru life when times were rough

Of education formal in life

I'm sure I've had enough

Yet save by twelve years while a child

All my time I've worked and toiled

My college years at Hard Knocks spent

Learning death, hunger, want and shame to toil

On graduation I received an ME

Much Experiences is what it meant

Then onwards I to University of Life

My entire adulthood to spend

The Pride-Honesty-Dependability degree

In ten short years I'd achieved

Without a handout loan or grant

Welfare unemploy or penny thieve

My fares and dues were always paid

Each one full and in advance

With silver sweat off of my brow

And golden calluses off my hands

I've talked with kings and learned men

I've spoke to o'er educated fools

I've never from a man's eyes looked

I've lived by the golden rule

I've eaten ne'er idle bread

I've slept no night in borrowed bed

I've earned the clothes upon my back

I've painted in pain the grey upon my head

I've been a help and friend to all

I've tried no man e'er to judge

I've taken each human at their worth

I've in humanity tried all to touch

So one day soon in honour I

Shall stand with others to receive

The highest mark education gives

The coveted doctorate degrees

Then before my name the DR there

My qualifications to all shall attest

As I in peace filled death shall lie

Granted at last my Deserved Rest

Some Fancy University

For 'less you've been to SFU

To them you have no brains

I've never been to SFU

But I'm happier just the same

For 'less you've been to SFU

To them you have no brains

I've never been to SFU

But I'm happier just the same

"Ne Dha Wha La Wan"

Nestled snug on Karen Island
But a stone's throw from Mainland shore
Mixed like a soup pot cosmopolitan
Each race and tribe there endure
Eeking out a bare existence
Dragging rich bags to the bank
Living squalid on welfare's pension
Or in splendour high o'erlooking the land
Faces bronzed, beaten, cut, tortured
Faces twisted from birth or fate's hand
Pale and white fat or scrawny
Ages all shared woman and man
Smell of fish when one wind bloweth
Pulp mill stench on opposing breeze
Warm thru rainfalls wet in Summer
Then nine months held in Winter's freeze
Hub on coast for north civilization
Terminus where huge cruisers pause
Place to hunt to fish to enjoy nature
Place to visit with or without cause
Nestled snug low behind its mountain
Kissed upon shores by salty tide
Host to nationals all north traveling

Home to those with adventurous pride
Cascading sea oft brow of seiner
Spray of wave of ferry ship
Roll of train along coastal railings
Chug of fish boat starting new trip
Calm of sunsets golden paints of Nature
Soothing call of birds 'cross waters still
Silent flight of lone bald-eagle searching
Sharp of eye and talon for a kill
Ages past cultures and generations
Indian tribes of many here are found
Some retain their bronze hued complexion
Other mixed with white black yellow brown
Thus like one great and family people
Live and seem peoples here you meet
Where today's technologies advances mingle
In contentment on for yesterday's street
Nestle safe snug on Karens Island
Saying welcome in the Tsimpsean tongue
Ne dha wha La Wan calls you to Prince Rupert
Genuine warmth assured all those who come
"Ne dha wha la wan" Prince Rupert Hello"

Shocks

Shock - You were pushed out into a world wherein your mothers peoples branded you a half breed

Shock - You as a toddler learn that throughout life you'll pay for some past unknown action word or deed

Shock - An infant yet you realize your father tho so proud lives as a beaten man

Shock - A young child now rejected degraded despised and you can't it understand

Shock - Another half breed enters in your young life as your brother

Shock - Two years pass by and from nowhere comes along yet still another

Shock - Strangers yet your blood and kindred you soon learn to love

Shock - So soon a unit knit so closely you've become now one

Shock - Now nine and happy you swing out carefree and glad

Shock - Listen clearly dear - Your mother died today words coming from your dad (shock - shock - shock)

Shock - Alone inside teenaged but yet a solitary lovelorn searching child

Shock - fifteen of age, again at last plays on your face traces of a smile

Shock - The scream of rubber tangled metal glass and broken bones

Shock - Your brother deep loved since birth in fatal useless crash is gone

Shock - Eighteen at last a woman full you've become or so to many it doth seem

Shock - E'en now you see no end or answer to the pain and sufferings that's been

Shock - Out in the world you find that tho a true native child of this land you and your people be

Shock - You realize that they like you have no voice, no help, no freedom it seems alas no destiny

Shock - Your fight back to better life for your native fellowmen

Shock - At twenty you lie beaten raped and pregnant with child who like you must live thru it all again (shock - shock - shock)

Still - Now not in shock at last you know you must not cut now short your life

For thru it all you've lived with hope dignity, and dreams of a recall to your burning Indian's pride.

There's A Ring Upon A Finger

There's a ring upon a finger

That's been moved from left to right

Tho significant it yet remains

It's a tiny golden circle

Light in weight and unadorned

Still it holds a lifelong story

Told in love, hurts 'n' pains it's known

For the circle rests unbroken

In one endless piece it winds

Like at first we were meant to do

Then it stood for joy and laughter

Then it stood for love and trust

Then it stood fore'er for me and you

But our circle has been shattered

And our world's been torn apart

Like disaster natural at night

Now the token of our feelings

Is all that here remains

Sitting where it moved from left to right

Sit and twirl it slowly softly

Listen to the voice it speaks

A recording of our lives it out plays

Just a simple golden circle
Which shouldn't mean so much
Yet on it is chronicled
Our every last minute detail
See the moment when we first met
And the way you held my hand
As we walk along our favourite street
See the friends we made all greet us
And the dreams that did come true
And the way we fight each obstacle we meet
See the tiny little cottage there
Where we slept upon the floor
For no beds save love could we afford
Feel the warmth which yet round lingers
From ceiling down to basement floor
And the love bursting from each door
Listen close now to the soft coos
As our firstborn lies awake
Playful clone in crib from auction mall
Hear his laughter childish giggles
E'en then I'm sure we knew
In our lives he'd play a leading part
Come and watch now all the pictures

As each day in scene is set
That not one moment lost to us may be
See the good times made from nothing
Save our care and toil and love
See us sitting by our own first Christmas tree
Flip along and roll the ring around
To a couple years ahead
As so full again with child you be
Then the morning of the brightest
Day man has of late seen
As yourself in miniature by you soft cry
Curls and laughter eyes of wonder
So like you in all most ways
Now together we four shall forever be
Roll the ring then see the years past
Stop now tell me if you can
Where began the fall of you and me
Now tell me
As you sit alone each weekend
While our children call me Dad
Does your thoughts and memories wander
To the good times which we had
Is the glow there in your eyes

Which like your tiny diamonds shine

A burning for what used to be

Or is it just memories of mine

As we say hello so casual

Does your look a message bear

Can our thought by the other still be read

Are there words which you'd like to share???

We could meet I say inside

And it's written in my face

But in our worlds of broken pride

To speak aloud might mean disgrace

Do you twirl your tiny ring too

Glance back into time as I

Or do you merely sit in emptiness

Happier now we've said goodbye

I've a thought to send you now

As always you're a part of me

Like the ring I wear unbroken is

So too is my lasting love for thee

Now I've said my piece completely

And so I'll walk off by myself

In the hope that soon you'll come to return

The ring back from right to left

<u>Players All Are We</u>

Players -- Aye just players
Players all are we
Like pegs on a game board called life
Like dice about to be shaken and thrown
Like white-eyed hard black dominoes
Like tokens on a gaming card
Like cards shuffled in a deck
So we on the game of life remain
Just players just pawns
Objects for the use works and enjoyment
Those graduated players
Who no longer like we are stand above as
Forgetful of the time like us they too
Stood steadfast e'er in readiness
For their number to be called
As players aye just players
Metamorphosis sets in
And we become hardened
Even harder than we were before
Like stone - like petrified bone
Like useless shale upon a shore
So hard are we that at the slightest provocation
Into tiny sharp barks we fly out

To strike down our aggravators
As our seemingly invincible shield
Our outwards appearance of hardness
Our shell built as self-protection
It falls apart and we break
Aye we break we fall asunder
Like clay pieces on a board
Like glass chessmen in a game
Like an egg shelled tennis ball that's hit
We revert again to substandard
We revert back to jelly likeness
We revert to our pre-catalytic state
As our cocoon fails to lend support
We revert again to be like players
Like players playing out life's game
Like players pawns upon a stage
Puppet like and regimented we stand
Male yes yet far now from man
Far from the maker's destiny now are we
Mere players in a never ending game
Mere players we in the charade called life
Players aye -- just players
Players all are we.

'Twas A Balmy Spring Day

'Twas a balmy spring day such as this
That I remember well
With soft fluffy clouds scattered
Like sheep across a blue grass meadow
With heaven itself the new earth which lent support to
This reversal of scenes in my mind
Lazy smoke curled upwards
From the distant smelly fish plant
Then stopped as if uncertain which route to take and so
Spreading out it forms a listless cloud of its own
Uncaring to destroy
The clear wool-like finish which floats above
The green glassy finish of the waters
Now the heavens of my mind
I've cut asunder as lighting flashes of birds appear
As thunder breaks its stillness and its mirror is
shattered
By passing boats which ripple and are gone
Then calm returns to the gossamer heaven like waters
As white winged angels fly across its mirrored surface
Checking full their wings and their heavenly attire
Before soaring onwards outwards
To that blue green meadow

Far beyond and with no place it seems of origination
The celestial voices of children sweet is heard in song
A break, a pause and clear out stands their leader
A soft voice sweet melodies and then is gone
Again the chorus the celestial chorus it rings across
Both heaven and sky is filled with cheer
The presence of creation dawns clear in the mind
As a power far greater than ours fills instantaneously --
The entire new hemisphere

Pause For Poetry

As the sun sets o'er the waters
Of Canada's western shores
As the cool calm fall of night you see
Take a moment out to ponder
Reflect back life upon awhile
Come join us for a pleasant short Pause for Poetry

Come linger awhile with others
As their views fully they share
About life and love about you and me
Let long echo on their writing
All week deep there in your thought
Heard where you once took a Pause for Poetry

Beyond The Far And Blue Horizon

Beyond the far and blue horizon
I wonder if a sphere exists
I ponder if a catalyst of colours
Entwine together in a dark abyss
Can nature's stars that shine and twinkle
Lend form unto a spectrum up above
Can meteorites that flash so fickle
Be sparklers of the heavens of his love
What wets the air and dew drops causes
To glitter soft upon a distant land
Or do these beauties far beyond us
Mean naught 'cept to the eyes of man
Beyond the far and blue horizon
Can sounds be heard do dreams appear
Or are these just within our visions
Unknown elsewhere with no one else to stare
Does set of sun a golden pathway wander
In purples, crimsons, reds and brown
And pale of moon bestowed on lovers
Do these leave naught as beyond they travel on
When time of sadness grabs our innards
And nature's balm is all that gives us ease
One wonders if beyond the far horizon

There are yet others who are blessed by these
Beyond the far and blue horizon
Is sitting yet we feel upon a throne
A master planner who did one time figure
Each water droplet each seedling and each stone
If such an architect as this did devise
Such untold splendour all for single man
Then vision all the unseen treasure
Which beyond the far horizon waits for man
Our sphere a dot in microscopic vision
Must surely 'fore his other work fast fade
Our splendour seen in all of nature
Must seem to them by far to be most pale
Yet we can sense the beauty and the power
As deep in awe our minds can't comprehend
The vastness there beyond the far horizon
Which separates for now the Gods and Men
But soon beyond that far and blue horizon
We'll be seeing light and we can enter in
To marvel in eternal wide eyed wonder
When all we become as one with God again

__Tiny White Cylinder__

Tiny white cylinder
So filled with lingering death
Why do you tempt me ever
Why try to take my breath
Your hot glowing fire ember
Turns dark as you I press
'Tween my lips in such hunger
As in my fingers you I caress
And as your ember darkens
It brings to my mind life
With death which constantly harkens
To follow our short bright life
So as you cigarette I ponder
While I am tempted for a smoke
What's your purpose in life I wonder
As my death seems your only joke
You destroy and corrupt my insides
You lead me a life of pain
While I suffer my cough reminds
Me, never to touch you again
But alas I am fast in your clutches
And for me long gone now is hope
As an addict I'm fast in your clutches
Of tar, nicotine and dope
So burn on you tiny reminder
As to a deaf world you do try to tell
That your burning only shows your partaker
That a burnt life leads only to hell

Ah Life What Has Thou Done

Ah life what has thou done
What has been done to thee by me
That seems as ever now
We too at variance are
Has prehaps some thought of mine
Some word my lips didst speak
Or mayhap yet some action I
Have caused which pain brought thee
If so then life speak out
For mercy's sake and for peace of mind
Speak out and let my troubled days
My sleepless restless endless nights
But for existence some rest find
Release me -- I beseech thee life
Release thy grip upon my carcass
And let it plunge into the deep abyss
Wherefrom it comest long ago
Let my now useless oils run out
Until my veins are empty fuel lines
Until an airlock ceases palpitation
Of the pump which thru me courses you
Ah life if I can nay forgiven be
Then do not but prolong my fate

Hang not then onto uncertainty
But release the coils of toil
The electric flashes sent by you
To power yet my dying cells
And to program me that I compute
Cut short the uselessness I feel
The great surround which envelopes
The aura of such dread nothingness
The useless meaning of unfinishable toil
Ah life what then has been done
What dark and dreary act of mine to you
Do you e'en now recall recall
Recall recall until you do react
And I a helpless gnat in thy hand
Unaware what for to make thee restitution
Can fain but linger on unliving
Like some vast catalyst or cocoon
Certain that life once moved within
Yet uncertain of what wait e'en now
Uncertain of what waits beyond tomorrows
And yet I must go on and on
For strength to stay thy will
Alas I have no longer here oath
I have no more of joy

No more of love or need or hope
I have no more of naught but this
That you as unto you I do beseech
Release me let me fall on back
Back back to the earthly dust
Back to the ashes and the dust
Wherefrom I came thru you
Let me regress into thy bosom
Let me fall back into oblivion
Let me return to folds of youth
Or else of thee I beg oh life
Free me my body spirit soul
MY mind my thoughts my will my all
Free me from all my wretchedness
And let my heart be joy filled
Let thy presence be once again
With vibrant meaning filled
Filled with the exuberant joy I knew
When you and I as one did co-exist
When you and I did please the world
When you oh life and I we lived
We lived we lived united

Once Again You're Painting

Once again you're painting the skyline
With hues of red purple and gold
Another day is now ending
Once more drawn nearer thy time
One day like the sun slowly sinking
In the splendour of the beautiful West
My life in thy hand will return Lord
And at last my soul will know rest
You've given the hillside and waters
Such beauty even where shadows fall
But to mankind the worst of your creatures
Dear Lord you've given your all
Yet still like the waters so silent
Or the caves hidden deep in the hill
Tho you know where we are
We seem not to care
For the beauty and love You afford
Yet your patience is long and enduring
With man your creation so blessed
Oh help me my God to see thee
Afore I must take my long rest
Help me to live love and work Lord
In love and fear only of You
Keep my life fulfilled
My soul warmed by thy will
And lead me nearer at Sunset
Dear Lord to YOU

I Listened To A Man

I listened to a man, black, unknown,

As he walked across his land

While he called loud unto his God

Spoke straight out man to man

"Yeh, well Lord I owe you one

I guess for all that you've done

That tight spot that I just got out

I sure couldn't 'ave done alone

I really don't know at times

Just what you see in me

I'm sure that so often and again

You have second thoughts of me

Why heck I don't 'tend no church

Dress up fancy, kneel and pray

And many's the time your existence

I've 'most logically argued away

Still strange it is Lord, guess you know,

I keep up my faith in you

E'en tho I most times find it hard

To live life like you said to

Maybe Lord I'm just an ornery cuss

Who's so hard I must need be tried

And made to call upon your help
To kinda hold back my ego 'n' pride
I just dunno Lord, I really don't
See what you in me find
But I'm grateful that you still hear
When your help I seek to find
These trials and tribulations all
Could be but to help me grow
Or payments for your mercies given
Know Lord? I sure hope so
Just think of the mess I made
Since last you helped me out
Heck why you e'en bothered again
Is one thing I sure think about
But I can't full change now can I
I'm the same me just like you planned
A stubborn hard headed fool
Determined to have my way when I can
Well Lord as I said I owe you one
A big one too it is this time
So when you feel to come collect
Just reach out and gimme a sign
Nah nothing fancy like of old

When to great prophets you did speak

Just come again here in my dreams

Sometimes when I'm asleep

You know the way I mean Lord

You've come so, so oft before

To show me glimpses the future of

Before I'd entered that times door

Well Lord I thank you once again

And I'll be speaking to you real soon"

Then like he had just left a friend

He walked on whistling a tune

'Tis strange I thought as he left

How so few of us think this way

This simple straight out way he talked

Might 'ave been his way to pray

For who's to say that his God

Whom he spoke to like a friend

Didn't understand his deep deep love

And regrets for failing again

Since then I've often sat alone

Thought of churches and folks I knew

Yet all their preachings ne'er had

Half his power of getting thru

You And I Old Faithful Friend

Summertime draws to a close
And Autumn winds begin to blow
As from the lonely lovers eyes
Tear season now is Fall
The Sunshine of a Spring romance
Which sparked a blazing Summer tan
Must give way to the withering leaves
As love slips thru lovers hand
Yet you and I old faithful friend
We rest again as oft we've done
Watch as the fading daylight draws
Away – and loves passion fade
We who were once the players too
Who chanced, and tried yet remain
Ahead of the pack but not aloof
For we've too seen passion fade
A lively lady's smile grows dim
Her best laid plans they're naught
While he in spirits hide away
The pain with which he's fraught
Yet Seasons come and Seasons go
Through Winters cold to wait
For Springs first warmth to renew
The game of life and love we've played
Yet you and I old faithful friend
We remain unchanged by all
Loving deep each other silently
Thru Spring – Summer and Fall
Unmindful that we're getting old
Unfeeling as the Winters cold

20/9/91

In Memory Of Randy

To the memory of Randy's death in a forest camp in October 1978
(Son of Audrey and Morris "Boisy" Ebanks)

Oh hard and grim and hectic was his life
His joys and pleasures they were few
His steps along the pathways he walked
Were each one fully paid in due
Yet the sparkle of his smile it gave
His mother warmth and peace content
His father and his infant brethern
Long shall recall the moments spent
With family love hope and belief
This their only solace no save you
In this their time
of deep unparallelled grief for
He was called and Oh God he came
He you took without a thought
Without a warning or a reason
That we mere mortals comprehend
Some better reach to roam among
Some better table where to grace
Some finer role anew to play
Could these your plans have been
Maybe maybe but silent God
Solemn and so seem uncaring
How can thy praise mortals raise

When in deaths darkness you lie waiting
When trusting striving soul is cut
A life is short a dream unended
A struggle long now stayed suspended
In agony, in deep unclimaxed doubt
'Cause you in silent wisdom moved
To call a soul away back to its rest
But hark, prehaps its better this
Prehaps some other boy or girl
From fate worse you have rescued
Some vile and hideous role unseen
From this your chosen has been drawn
And saved forever in eternal rest
Tho mortal heart can fain but wonder
At thy works and ways they do manifest
When one so young so eager and so free
Is cut away from roots of livelihood
Like seasoned trunk cut from forest tree
Cut into finer bark and wood and chips
Than visibly did appear to mortal we
So stay instead our thoughts of painful doubt
Soothe full our anguished hearts and minds
Let reason yours alone to out exact
Slow enter till thy peacefulness we find
Slow enter till thy act of deeper love
Can fill our lives o'er all the painfulness
And thru thy wisdom we consoled can lie

For is not death itself another door
Wherein a pinnacle higher we attain
A blending point of man and God
A release to enter into heavens realm
If it be not then God this knowledge keep
Let life's ebb more of a meaning hold
Than just a void filled of unwaking sleep
Or a precipice o'erlooking deaths dark door
Lend meaning to this loss of son of man
Struck down in youth among thy forest glade
In toil for sustenance your temple to sustain
As in faith thy hands into we his body lay
While helplessly his life so short is thru
Pray balance out his many works and deeds
With those owed yet Lord unto you for
Hard and grim and hectic was his life
His joys and pleasures they were few
His steps along the pathways he did walk
Were each one fully paid in due
Were each one Lord fully paid in due
Yet the sparkle of his smile it gave
His mother warmth and peace content
His father and his infant brethern
Long shall recall the moments spent
With family love hope and belief
This their only solace no save you
In this their time of deep unparallelled grief

A Charmer No No Charmer I

A charmer no no charmer I
So do not call me so
'Tis but reaction passing by
When e'er you by I go
For oft it's been this way before
When two have met awhile
One captured by the speaking eye
Or by the winning smile
Or yet mayhap 'tis but a word
Which quick and soft 'twas spoken
That caused a heart to palpitate
Tho so oft before 'twas broken
I know not care not
Let it be
Let's let life pass us by
You the ultimate of desirability
And plain non charmer I

No charmer I oh no not me
For obliged we both doth seem
Tho it may but be protective force
Or hopes of a waiting dream
We each may hide behind a mask

Our truth of loneliness to stay
Reaching out in snide cutting remarks
Seemingly happy in our play
Yet deep within a fire burns
Which rages to be free
'Tis this that looks you towards
'Cross chasms 'twix you and me

'The most desirable' says a lot
Sums what you make one feel
'Tis not then a charmer I
But what you bring out in me
So walk away far from my life
For danger deep in you lurks
Enchantment which an evening brings
Followed by lone life of hurts
Too much is seen within your eyes
To long resist if you demand
A captive soon to be of yours
Your every wish but my command
So walk away call no charmer me
Return to your lair I pray
Take your charm, warmth, desirability
Tempt not me to come your way

Other Collections By This Author

A Poet's Ebb And Flow

. . . and Touches Of Nature

In The Middle Of BeLIEve There's A Lie (Song Lyrics)

Inside A Heart

Judge Me Not Without A Trial

Legends, Lives & Loves Along the Inside Passage

Love... Life's Illusive Zenith

Love's Reflections

Love's Refuge and Sonnets

Only Children Of The Universe Are We

That We Too Free May Live

~ ~

For more information go to:

w w w . d n c s i t e . c a

~ ~

www.ingramcontent.com/pod-product-compliance
Lightning Source LLC
Chambersburg PA
CBHW070052120426
42742CB00048B/2404